Mary Magdalene

The Hidden Illumined One

Edited by

Theodore J. Nottingham

© 2014 Theodore J. Nottingham

ISBN 978-1502415042

Cover art by Richard Stodart

Printed in the United States of America.

Table of Contents

1

The Journey of Mary Magdalene

Mary Magdalene is portrayed by the Church as a prostitute who was redeemed by her love for the Anointed One. However, neither the Eastern Orthodox traditions nor the Gnostic traditions portray her in this way. The labeling of Magdalene as a prostitute originated with Pope Gregory the Great when he issued Homily 33 in 591 AD. Gregory claimed that the seven devils that Jesus cast out of Magdalene were the seven deadly sins, and reinterpreted her act of washing Jesus' feet with her tears and drying them with her hair.

Gregory asserted that Mary Magdalene, Mary, sister of Martha and Lazarus of Bethany, and the unnamed sinner in Luke who anoints Christ's feet were all the same person (Haskins 16). And although the Catholic Church officially redacted this decree in 1969, his depiction of Mary Magdalene is still believed by many as the "Gospel Truth"). The power of one pope to change the world's perception of a Biblical character, hundreds of years after the fact, and for over a thousand years into the future, gives one pause for thought.

In reality, little is known for certain about Mary Magdalene. Even the origin of her name is unclear. Magdalene may indicate that she came from the town of Magdala (Migdal), located on the west shore of the Sea of Galilee (Lake Gennesaret) just north of Tiberias. (Other sources agree with Pope Gregory that she was from Bethany.) Still others argue that Magdala means "tower, magnificent, or great," and that calling her Mary Magdalene is like calling her "Mary the Great." But, either way, she is presented as an independent woman— by place of birth or nobleness of being—rather than by husband or other male relationship as was usual at the time. This, in itself, is a clue to her strength, power, and uniqueness.

When perusing the Bible to learn more about Mary

Magdalene, we find that the synoptic Gospels do not give a lot of detail on her life. But according to Leloup, they do agree on four points:

* She was one of Christ's female followers.

* She was present at the crucifixion.

* She was the witness of his resurrection.

* She was the first to be charged with the supreme ministry of proclaiming the Christian message.

Additionally, Mary's name is placed first six of the seven times the women who followed Jesus are listed. And, in the Gospel of John, the risen Jesus gives her special teachings and commissions her to announce the good news of the resurrection to the other disciples, for which she is often called the "Apostle to the Apostles." The Gospel of Luke identifies her as one "from whom seven demons had gone out." This reference to a cleansing has none of the moral judgment that Pope Gregory later attached to it, but can be open to other interpretations. For example, it could just as easily be postulated that her seven chakras were opened by being in the presence of

Jesus. Similar transformations are documented of those who reached enlightenment in the presence of the Buddha.

In the Gnostic Gospels, we find that Mary Magdalene is shown as a prominent disciple of Jesus. Instances of this exalted status are found in the Gospel of Thomas, First Apocalypse of James, Dialogue of the Savior, Sophia of Jesus Christ, the Gospel of Philip, and the Pistis Sophia, as well as the Gospel of Mary from the Berlin Codex. These works portray Mary as one of the participants in the dialogues between Jesus and his disciples. She is clearly a member of His inner group and well-able to articulate the teachings to those who have trouble understanding them. For example, in Dialogue of the Savior, the narrator confirms "she uttered this as a woman who had understood completely."

The Gospel of Mary presents her as a leader among the disciples. She does not fear for her life after Jesus' death, but goes forth and visits the tomb of Jesus, while the rest of the disciples hide in a locked chamber in fear of the authorities. The Savior praises Mary for her unwavering steadfastness. She experiences a vision of Jesus and receives advance teaching about the fate of the soul and salvation. It is this vision that she shares in her Gospel, which is unfortunately incomplete. Still, it is clear from this Gospel that she was a comforter and instructor to the other disciples, some of whom respected her in this role and some of whom challenged her authority.

During the sixth century, many legends of Mary Magdalene were created. It was around this time that the last temple of the goddess was closed, and the Catholic Church officially outlawed goddess worship. It was also during this time that Pope Gregory delivered the sermon that redefined her in terms more compatible with his vision of the role of the feminine in the Church. Some legends say that Mary Magdalene was a powerful preacher for a short period after Christ's death. As she was contemplative by nature, she soon retired to a cave where she fasted for thirty years, being borne up by angels everyday for spiritual sustenance. Little was heard of her for centuries. But in the twelfth century, with the rise of the grail legends, the worship of Mary Magdalene again became prevalent and churches claiming to have a relic of her flourished.

2

Legends and Oral Tradition

On the shores of the Mediterranean Sea outside
Marseilles at Les Saintes Marie de la Mere there is a small
chapel dedicated to Mary Magdalene and consecrated by
Archbishop Roncalli (who later became Pope John
XXIII). Given a place of prominence within this chapel
are paintings of her arrival from Palestine in a small
rudderless boat. According to legend, soon after the
crucifixion and Resurrection, Mary Magdalene and her
family were expelled from the Holy Land, set adrift on
the Mediterranean Sea and made their way to this region,
particularly the area around Southern France and
Northern Spain.

Here, according to an ancient French legend, Mary
Magdalene landed in a small boat around 42 CE, along

with a number of early Christians, including a young, dark-skinned servant named Sarah, patron saint of the gypsies and often equated with the black Madonna statues in the churches of France. They had braved a dangerous passage from the Holy Land, without sails and oars, to spread Jesus's teachings after his Crucifixion. Purportedly a great preacher in Palestine who even wrote her own Gospel (among the more recently discovered esoteric Gnostic texts being studied by scholars), Magdalene is said to have preached to the locals in Saintes-Maries, converting many.

At this time in history, aside from the already established Celts, many Greeks, Arabs, Jews and others lived and travelled in this area. There was even a Jewish city known as Glanum Levi whose ruins can be found today in Provence.

In the midst of this cosmopolitan confluence of cultures, along with the exchange of goods there must have been an exchange of philosophical and religious ideas. It is very possible that during this period many spiritual and symbolic links were discovered between these diverse peoples and their traditional belief systems that stretched back to the temples of Egypt. Before her arrival in Les Saintes Marie Sur Les Mere, France was riddled with Isis cults. The name Paris etymologically can be linked to the pre-Celtic *ParIsis*, the grove of Isis. Clearly this region was fertile ground for Mary Magdalene's mission. Following her arrival in France, she was said to have travelled the land, preaching the authentic Gnostic gospel of Jesus, which had been directly transmitted to her during his time on Earth and in mystic visions after his return to the more subtle dimensions of light. French religious literature from the Middle Ages is filled with legends and stories of the life of Mary Magdalene from this period until her death. Tales abound of her miraculous healings, her performance of the ritual of baptism, her aid in fertility and childbearing and even her ability to raise the dead. There are even reports of a secret tradition of the healing arts that exists today in France and traces its roots back to Mary Magdalene.

After this prophetic mission was accomplished, Mary is

reported to have withdrawn to a cave in Ste. Baum, where she spent the remainder of her days in pray and seclusion. She is believed to have been buried at Sainte Maximin where her remains were watched over by Cassianite monks from the fifth century until the Saracen invasion. Then in 1058, in a papal bull, Pope Stephen acknowledged the existence of her relics in the church of Vezeley, which became one of the major places of pilgrimage during the Middle Ages.

But before we look at the evidence for her distinctive role as Apostle of the Apostles and prophetic mission, let us take a look at the hidden history of Gnosticism, the powerful doctrine of Divine grace, healing and illumination that she was said to have transmitted.

The Gnostic Teachings

It was during the Hellenistic period that the mystic knowledge of Egypt, the great symbols, myths, astronomical, scientific and metaphysical teachings passed into the heart of the Mystery Schools of Greece and Rome, which included the region of Gaul where Mary Magdalene is reported to have lived and preached. These secret initiatory teachings of the Egyptians were also retained and transmitted through the inner circles of Judaism to Jesus himself.

At the heart of this lineage of transmission was an extraordinary metaphysical teaching known as Gnosticism. This teaching is believed to be the spiritual basis of his essential message to humanity, a message revealed to Mary Magdalene, his disciples and followers through the vehicles of metaphor, allegory and parable. Unlike the patriarchal, dogmatic, materially based teachings prevalent during this period, Gnosticism placed primary value on the feminine qualities of receptivity, intuitive perception, visionary experience and the art of healing. It was a teaching of love, selflessness, harmony and communion.

The mystic experience of, and communion with, the essential grace and majesty of Divinity, lay at the heart of this Gnostic transmission. The clear and immediate experience of this awakening was known as *gnosis* or wisdom. Often translated from its Greek root as 'knowledge', Gnosticism goes much deeper than mere intellectual understanding. Like a brilliant flash of light arising from the darkness, this understanding arises in the individual as a bright lucid awareness – an intuitive realisation of the pure essence, nature and energy of Divinity as it flows within oneself, the luminous realms and all of creation.

From the Gnostic viewpoint, the answers to all of life's mysteries can only be found when one "opens oneself to this divine current and allows oneself to be penetrated by it to the point where one is fully transformed and illuminated by it." From the viewpoint of many early Gnostic communities, this divine current was perceived as the feminine, healing and nurturing energy of God's Holy Spirit.

The fundamental doctrine of the Gnostics relates the dualistic nature of the world in which we reside, the eternal struggle between good and evil. They believed that Jehovah, the wrathful god of the Old Testament was a false god and expression of what they called the *demiurge*. For how could a fully enlightened divinity contain within him the base emotions of anger, jealousy and vengeance? For them, the real God was a loving deity equally and directly accessible to all. This God taught that love, compassion and the true sacrifice and transformation of the self, or ego, was the highest spiritual path.

The Gnostics believed that the plan of this *demiurge*, or Satan, was to trap spirit in matter, and the Earth itself was a prison in which souls were exiled from their divine home. For them, the real world was the non-material world of spirit and all of their rituals and practices were designed to purify them and provide them with the means to find their way out of the impure world of matter, darkness and suffering and return to their true home in the Light.

Clearly, these sacred esoteric teachings were revolutionary. Unlike the fixed, restrictive, hierarchical systems prevalent during this period, these teachings were open to all, female, male, rich, poor Jew or Pagan. This all-inclusive transmission of teachings formerly reserved for the elite was at odds with the practices of Orthodox Judaism and the emerging Church of Rome. For once the seeker had been touched by this Gnostic current, she or he came to recognise their own divine nature and perceive their place in the world from a whole new perspective. No longer did they need the intercession of a priest or rabbi to connect them with their spiritual inheritance.

Evidence of Mary Magdalene's primary role as disciple, visionary, mediatrix and herald of these revolutionary teachings can be found in a number of Gnostic texts. These include *The Pistis Sophia, The Gospel of Philip, The Gospel of Mary* and more.

Apostle of the Apostles

The *Pistis Sophia* is a Coptic Gnostic revelatory work composed and/or compiled in Egypt around the middle of the second century CE. It claims to disclose the "secret teachings of the Savior," reserved for his inner circle of initiates during the eleven years following his

Resurrection. Filled with powerful, poetic imagery, this text reveals the intimate connections between this emerging form of Christianity, Paganism and beliefs and rituals founds in the Egyptian Book of the Dead. It also clearly recognizes and demonstrates Mary Magdalene's essential role as foremost disciple, seer and prophetess.

It appears the teachings found in the *Pistis Sophia* were created specifically for the apostles who would go forth and spread his gospel. It takes the form of a dialogue between Jesus and these apostles and consists primarily of questions and answers. It is fascinating to note that in this text, out of the forty-six questions asked of him, thirty-nine of them come from Mary Magdalene. Due to her sincerity, astute level of inquiry and ability to comprehend the essence of his words, time and time again she is praised and recognized by him for her clarity and insight.

For example, after Jesus presents the first part of these mystical teachings concerning the aeons, orders and regions of the "Great Invisible," he acknowledges Mary Magdalene's superior capacity for contemplation, insight and revelation.

It came to pass then, when Mary had heard the Savior say these words, that she gazed fixedly into the air for the space of an hour. She said: "My Lord, give commandment to me to speak in openness." And Jesus, the compassionate, answered and said unto Mary:

"Mary, thou blessed one, whom I will perfect in all mysteries, of those of the height, discourse in openness, thou, whose heart is raised to the Kingdom of Heaven more than all thy brethren."

Throughout the text, after listening to her interpretation of his teachings, he acknowledges her perceptive abilities:

Well, said, Mary, for thou art blessed before all women on earth, because thou shalt be the fullness of all fullness and the perfection of all perfections.

This is only the first of a number of texts that speak of Mary Magdalene's gifts and unique relationship with Jesus. According to a group of Gnostic Gospels discovered in 1945 in a cave in Upper Egypt near the village of Nag Hammadi, she was said to be an inspired prophetess who continuously experienced the living presence of her Lord within her.

In *The Gospel of Mary*, from this collection, Mary Magdalene, the visionary, reveals to the other disciples teachings that were transmitted to her through visionary experience. In this gospel, she clearly takes the lead, not only soothing and reassuring the male apostles who fear capture and death, but relating to them teachings of the Savior that she alone has been privileged to receive. As in the *Pistis Sophia*, the Savior blesses her for her visionary capacity. When Peter questions her vision, Levi responds with, "If the Teacher held her worthy, who are you to reject her? Surely the Teacher knew her very well, for he loved her more than us."

In *The Gospel of Philip*, from the same collection, the disciples appear to be jealous of the intimate relationship between the Savior and Mary Magdalene.

The Companion of the savior is Mary Magdalene. But Christ loved her more than all the disciples and used to kiss her often on the mouth. The rest of the disciples were offended by it and expressed disapproval. They said to him, "Why do you love her more than all of us?" The Savior answered and said to them, "Why do I not love you like her? When a blind man and one who sees are both together in darkness, they are no different from one another. When the light comes then he who sees will see the light, and he who is blind will remain in darkness."

The Christianity brought to France by Mary Magdalene has a different feel about it because it seems closer to the authentic teachings of Jesus. If Mary Magdalene truly was the Apostle of the Apostles, then Jesus transmitted more to her or perhaps she understood this transmission better than the rest of the apostles. Through this lens we can begin to perceive and acknowledge the different understanding and practice of Christianity that emerged in Southern France, one that lasted over 1,200 years and in a sense pervades the place to this day.

Magdalene's Legacy

When one looks at the history of the region of southern France one finds evidence that with her arrival, a surge of spiritual awareness, code of ethics and respect for feminine values began, which wove itself into the very fabric of the psychic landscape of Europe. The Order of the Knights Templar was created in this region. The alchemists began their flurry of Cathedral building to preserve the secret metaphysical teachings passed down to them from ancient Egypt. The Crusades and the entire Back to Jerusalem movement began in this area. The mystical Kabbalistic texts the *Bahir* and *Zohar* emerged from this region, bringing to the Jewish people knowledge of the Shekhina, or 'indwelling presence' and 'feminine potency of God'. The cults of the Virgin Mary, Mary Magdalene and Black Madonna, symbolically representing the three aspects of Isis in her role as Universal Goddess, arose here and spread throughout Europe.

It was here the troubadours and poets such as Wolfram von Eschenbach, Robert de Bouron and others sang their songs of devotion to the feminine principle and wrote their fables of the Holy Grail. And it was here in the beautiful mountains and valleys of Provence and Languedoc that the Cathars, as carriers of the Gnostic transmission of Jesus and Mary Magdalene, rebelled against what they considered to be the excesses of the priestly hierarchy, renounced all worldly possessions and fully committed themselves to the path of spirit. Among the Cathars, women as well as men were priests who transmitted divine grace and healing power through the laying on of hands in their sacred initiatory rites that link back to Mary Magdalene, Isis and the healing traditions held by the temple priestess.

As time marched on, the Church of Rome, threatened by the inroads these powerful Gnostic teachings were making among the local populace, labelled them heretical and moved to suppress them. To cement the rule of the Church of Rome, Pope Innocent III called for a Crusade against this Gnostic Cathar heresy. This crusade, which had as its focus the torture, murder and eradication of these loving and compassionate people was the starting point of a wave of fear, suffering and suppression of the feminine in both her divine and worldly aspects that would spread throughout Europe and become known as the Holy Inquisition.

Closer to our time, there are the visions of Saint Bernadette and the healing waters of Lourdes, as well as the mystery of Father Sauniere, Rennes Le Chateau and his strange chapel dedicated to Mary Magdalene. Then there is the saga of Otto Rahn searching through the hills and valleys of this region for the Nazis trying to find the Holy Grail for the upper echelon of the SS. There are the legends of the secret alchemists who live in a magical castle somewhere in the Pyrenees recently popularised in the Harry Potter series. Finally, emerging from this region, is the mystery of the Alchemical Cross of Hendaye, the prophetic visions of Nostradamus and the Basque legend that John of the Apocalypse still lives in a cave in the Pyrenees and will leave that cave only at the end of time.5

These events and stories reveal that Mary Magdalene and the Gnostic current may very possibly be the driving force behind the rich history of this region. Whether it is fact or legend that Mary Magdalene actually came to this area is less important than the power and impact her life and teachings had upon the people of France. It is obvious to anyone who opens their eyes to see, that early in the history of this grace-filled tradition, Mary Magdalene, Apostle of the Apostles entered and has remained at the heart of Christianity.

3

The Mystery of Mary Magdalene

Other legends, especially in Provence, France, celebrated her as the mother of Jesus' daughter, Sarah. Sarah may be a title rather than a name as it means "queen" or "princess" in Hebrew. In Les-Saintes-Maries-de-la-Mer, France, there is an annual festival from May 23 to 25 at a shrine dedicated to St. Sarah the Egyptian, also called Sarah Kali, the Black Queen. This festival originated in the Middle Ages, and is **in honor of an** Egyptian child said to have been brought over by Mary Magdalene, Martha, and Lazarus in 42 AD. Sarah is symbolically black because she is a secret and that only the initiated may know her true origin. There is speculation that the Black Madonnas, which were created over a span from the fifth to the twelfth centuries, and are still venerated

27

in Poland, Spain, Germany, France, Czechoslovakia and other European countries, are really depictions of Mary Magdalene and Sarah, rather than the traditional Madonna and Child. Some proponents of this theory say there is evidence that the royal bloodline of Jesus and Mary Magdalene flowed in the Merovingian monarchs of France. Merovingian breaks down into "Mer" or "Mary" or "the sea," and "vin" for "the vine." So it can mean "vine of Mary" or "vine of the mother" possibly representing the bloodline of Mary Magdalene and Jesus.

In twelfth-century Europe, there was a strong appreciation of the feminine, especially in Provence, where women held fief and manor by right of inheritance as early as the tenth century. The cult of Mary Magdalene heralded her as the patron saint of gardens and vineyards, the mediator of fertility, beauty and the joy of life. She filled the role of the love goddess of antiquity. During this time, Jerusalem was recaptured, and the Order of the Knights Templar, which has become well-known through *The Da Vinci Code*, flourished.

The legends of Mary, and other esoteric teachings were later forced underground by the Church through the ruthless torture of the Papal Inquisition which started in 1233. Mary Magdalene was again repressed and Mary, mother of Jesus, believed to be a virgin, was held up as the role model for women in the Church.

On the Gospel of Mary

Written early in the second century CE, it disappeared for over fifteen hundred years until a single, fragmentary copy in Coptic translation came to light in the late nineteenth century. Although details of the discovery itself are obscure, we do know that the fifth-century manuscript in which it was inscribed was purchased in Cairo by Carl Reinhardt and brought to Berlin in 1896. Two additional fragments in Greek have come to light in the twentieth century. Yet still no complete copy of the *Gospel of Mary is* known. Fewer than eight pages of the ancient papyrus text survive, which means that about half of the *Gospel of Mary* is lost to us, perhaps forever.

Yet these scant pages provide an intriguing glimpse into a kind of Christianity lost for almost fifteen hundred years. This astonishingly brief narrative presents a radical interpretation of Jesus' teachings as a path to inner spiritual knowledge; it rejects his suffering and death as the path to eternal life; it exposes the erroneous view that Mary of Magdala was a prostitute for what it is - a piece of theological fiction; it presents the most straightforward and convincing argument in any early Christian writing for the legitimacy of women's leadership; it offers a sharp critique of illegitimate power and a utopian vision of spiritual perfection; it challenges our rather romantic views about the harmony and unanimity of the first Christians; and it asks us to rethink the basis for church authority. All written in the name of a woman.

Since the first six pages are lost, the gospel opens in the middle of a scene portraying a discussion between the Savior and his disciples set after the resurrection. The

Savior is answering their questions about the end of the material world and the nature of sin. He teaches them that at present all things, whether material or spiritual, are interwoven with each other. In the end, that will not be so. Each nature will return to its own root, its own original state and destiny. But meanwhile, the nature of sin is tied to the nature of life in this mixed world. People sin because they do not recognize their own spiritual nature and, instead, love the lower nature that deceives them and leads to disease and death. Salvation is achieved by discovering within oneself the true spiritual nature of humanity and overcoming the deceptive entrapments of the bodily passions and the world. The Savior concludes this teaching with a warning against those who would delude the disciples into following some heroic leader or a set of rules and laws. Instead they are to seek the child of true Humanity within themselves and gain inward peace. After commissioning them to go forth and preach the gospel, the Savior departs.

But the disciples do not go out joyfully to preach the

gospel; instead controversy erupts. All the disciples except Mary have failed to comprehend the Savior's teaching Rather than seek peace within, they are distraught, frightened that if they follow his commission to preach the gospel, they might share his agonizing fate. Mary steps in and comforts them and, at Peter's, relates teaching unknown to them that she had received from the Savior in a vision. The Savior had explained to her the nature of prophecy and the rise of the soul to its final rest, describing how to win the battle against the wicked, illegitimate Powers that seek to keep the soul entrapped in the world and ignorant of its true spiritual nature.

But as she finishes her account, two of the disciples quite unexpectedly challenge her. Andrew objects that her teaching is strange and he refuses to believe that it came from the Savior. Peter goes further, denying that Jesus would ever have given this kind of advanced teaching to a woman, or that Jesus could possibly have preferred her to them. Apparently when he asked her to speak, Peter had not expected such elevated teaching, and now he questions her character, implying that she has lied about having received special teaching in order to increase her stature among the disciples. Severely taken aback, Mary begins to cry at Peter's accusation. Levi comes quickly to her defense, pointing out to Peter that he is a notorious hothead and now he is treating Mary as though she were the enemy. We should be ashamed of ourselves, he admonishes them all; instead of arguing among ourselves, we should go out and preach the gospel as the Savior commanded us.

The story ends here, but the controversy is far from resolved. Andrew and Peter at least, and likely the other fearful disciples as well, have not understood the Savior's teaching and are offended by Jesus' apparent preference of a woman over them. Their limited understanding and false pride make it impossible for them to comprehend the truth of the Savior's teaching. The reader must both wonder and worry what kind of gospel such proud and ignorant disciples will preach.

How are we to understand this story? It is at once reminiscent of the New Testament gospels and yet clearly different from them. The gospel's characters - the

Savior, Mary, Peter, Andrew, and Levi - are familiar to those acquainted with the gospels of *Matthew, Mark, Luke,* and *John. So,* too, is the theological language of gospel and kingdom, as well as such sayings of Jesus as "Those who seek will find" or "Anyone with two ears should listen." And the New Testament gospels and Acts repeatedly mention the appearance of Jesus to his disciples after the resurrection. Yet it is also clear that the story of the *Gospel of Mary* differs in significant respects. For example, after Jesus commissions the disciples, they do not go out joyfully to preach the gospel, as they do in *Matthew;* instead they weep, fearing for their lives. Some of the teachings also seem shocking coming from Jesus, especially his assertion that there is no such thing as sin. Modern re ad-ers may well find themselves sympathizing with Andrew's assessment that "these teachings are strange ideas."

The *Gospel of Mary* was written when Christianity, still in its early stages, was made up of communities widely dispersed around the Eastern Mediterranean, communities which were often relatively isola ted from one other and probably each small enough to meet in someone's home without attracting too much notice. Although writings appeared early - especially letters addressing the concerns of local churches, collections containing Jesus' sayings, and narratives interpreting his death and resurrection—oral practices dominated the lives of early Christians. Preaching, teaching, and rituals of table fellowship and baptism were the core of the Christian experience.

What written documents they had served at most as supplemental guides to preaching and practice. Nor can we assume that the various churches all possessed the same documents; after all, these are the people who wrote the first Christian literature. Christoph Markschies suggests that we have lost 85% of Christian literature from the first two centuries – and that includes only the literature we know about. Surely there must be even more, for the discovery of texts like the *Gospel of Mary* came as a complete surprise. We have to be careful that we don't suppose it is possible to reconstruct the whole of early Christian history and practice out of the few surviving texts that remain. Our picture will always be partial — not only because so much is lost, but because early Christian practices were so little tied to durable writing.

Partly as a consequence of their independent development and differing situations, these churches sometimes diverged widely in their perspectives on essential elements of Christian belief and practice. Such basic issues as the content and meaning of Jesus' teachings, the nature of salvation, the value of prophetic authority, and the roles of women and slaves came under intense debate. Early Christians proposed and experimented with competing visions of ideal community.

It is important to remember, too, that these first Christians had no New Testament, no Nicene Creed or Apostles Creed, no commonly established church order or chain of authority, no church buildings, and indeed no single understanding of Jesus. All of the elements we might consider to be essential to define Christianity did not yet exist. Far from being starting points, the Nicene creed and the New Testament were the end products of these debates and disputes; they represent the distillation of experience and experimentation—and not a small amount of strife and struggle.

All early Christian literature bears traces of these controversies. The earliest surviving documents of Christianity, the letters of Paul, show that considerable difference of opinion existed about such issues as circumcision and the Jewish food laws or the relative value of spiritual gifts. By the time of the *Gospel of Mary*, these discussions were becoming increasingly nuanced and more polarized.

4

The Discovery of the Gospel of Mary

From the beginning, the publication was plagued by difficulties. First of all, there is the problem of the missing pages. The first six pages, plus four additional pages from the middle of the work, are missing. This means that over half of the *Gospel of Mary* is completely lost. What happened to these pages? Carl Schmidt thought they must have been stolen or destroyed by whoever found the book. The manuscript itself was found protected inside its original leather and papyrus cover but by the time it reached Carl Schmidt in Berlin, the order of the pages had been considerably jumbled. It took Schmidt some time to realize that the book was nearly intact and must therefore have been found uninjured. Schmidt attributed the disorder of the pages to the local people who first found them and who must also have either stolen or destroyed the missing pages, but to this day nothing is known about their fate. We can only hope that they lie protected somewhere and will one day resurface.

By 1912 Schmidt's edition was ready for publication and was sent to the Prießchen Press in Leipzig. The printer was nearing completion of the final sheets when a burst water pipe destroyed the entire edition. Soon thereafter Europe plunged into World War I. During the war and its aftermath, Schmidt was unable to go to Leipzig and salvage anything from the mess himself, but he did manage to resurrect the project. This time, however, his work was thwarted by his own mortality. His death on April 17, 1938, caused further delay while the edition was retrieved from his estate and sent to press. At this point, another scholar was needed to see its publication through, a task that ultimately fell to Walter Till in 1941.

In the meantime, in 1917 a small third-century Greek fragment of the *Gospel of Mary* had been found in Egypt.

Being parallel to part of the Coptic text, it added no new passages to the *Gospel of Mary,* but it did provide a few variants and additional evidence about the work's early date and its composition in Greek. Till incorporated this new evidence into his edition, and by 1943, the edition was again ready to go to press. But now World War II made publication impossible.

By the time the war was over, news had reached Berlin of a major manuscript discovery in Egypt near the village of Nag Hammadi. As chance would have it, copies of two of the other texts found within the Berlin Codex along with the *Gospel of Mary (Apocryphon of John and Sophia of Jesus Christ)* appeared among the new manuscripts. No new copies of *Gospel of Mary* were found at Nag Hammadi, but publication was delayed yet again as Till waited for information about the new manuscripts so that he could incorporate this new evidence into his edition of the Berlin Codex. But the wheels of scholarship grind slowly, and finally in exasperation, Till gave up. He confides to his readers:

In the course of the twelve years during which I have

labored over the texts, I often made repeated changes here and there, and that will probably continue to be the case. But at some point a man must find the courage to let the manuscript leave one's hand, even if one is convinced that there is much that is still imperfect. That is unavoidable with all human endeavors.

At last in 1955, the first printed edition of the text of the *Gospel of Mary* finally appeared in a German translation.

Till was right, of course; scholars continue to make changes and add to the record. Of foremost importance was the discovery of yet another early third-century Greek fragment of the *Gospel of Mary*, which was published in 1983. With the addition of this fragment, we now have portions of three copies of the *Gospel of Mary* dating from antiquity: two Greek manuscripts from the early third century and one in Coptic from the fifth century.

Because it is unusual for several copies from such early dates to have survived, the attestation of the *Gospel of Mary* as an early Christian work is unusually strong. Most early Christian literature that we know about has survived because the texts were copied and then recopied as the materials on which they were written wore out. In antiquity it was not necessary to burn books one wanted to suppress (although this was occasionally done); if they weren't recopied, they disappeared through neglect. As far as we know, the *Gospel of Mary was* never recopied after the fifth century; it may have been that the *Gospel of Mary* was actively suppressed, but it is also possible that it simply dropped out of circulation. Either way, whether its loss resulted from animosity or neglect, the recovery of the *Gospel of Mary,* in however fragmentary condition, is due in equal measure to phenomenal serendipity and extraordinary good fortune.

The Teachings and Visions

Mary Magdalene is making her return, but it has been slow. In 1772, a fourth-century parchment was found (Codex Askewianis). It contained the Pistis Sophia, which features a dialogue that Jesus conducted with

Mary Magadelene and the other disciples. In 1896, a papyrus codex dating to the fifth century was found. It contained two texts entitled "Gospel of Mary" and "The Sophia of Jesus." In 1945, the Nag Hammadi texts, which contained several works that made mention of Mary, including a second "Sophia of Jesus" were discovered. Some early third century Greek fragments have supplemented both the "Gospel of Mary" and the "Gospel of Thomas," one of the Nag Hammadi texts. In 2003, Karen L. King, a Biblical scholar, published *Gospel of Mary of Magdala: Jesus and the First Woman Apostle,* which places the two extant fragments side by side. It is believed ten pages of the "Gospel of Mary" are still missing.

The following is an excerpt from the Gospel of Mary Magdalene found in the book *The Gospel of Mary of Magdala: Jesus and the First Woman Apostle* by Karen L. King. It describes the ascent of the soul to heaven by the severing of various ties to the earth. It describes one of the secret teachings that Christ gave to Mary Magdalene after his resurrection and picks up after a four-page gap in the original manuscript. In these four pages, the soul has conquered the first of the four powers. This power was probably named "Darkness." The excerpt begins when the soul is confronting the second power, "Desire."

And Desire said, 'I did not see you go down, yet now I see you go up. So why do you lie since you belong to me?'

The soul answered, 'I saw you. You did not see me nor did you know me. You mistook the garment I wore for my true self. And you did not recognize me.'

After it had said these things, it left rejoicing greatly

Again, it came to the third Power, which is called 'Ignorance.' It examined the soul closely, saying, 'Where are you going? You are bound by wickedness. Indeed you are bound! Do not judge!'

And the soul said, 'Why do you judge me, since I have not passed judgment? I have been bound, but I have not bound anything. They did not recognize me, but I have recognized that the universe is to be dissolved, both the things of earth and those of heaven.'

When the soul had brought the third Power to naught, it went upward and saw the fourth Power. It had seven forms. The first form is darkness, the second is desire; the third is ignorance; the fourth deadly envy; the fifth enslavement of the body; the sixth is the foolish wisdom of the flesh; the seventh is the wisdom of the wrathful person. These are the seven Powers of Wrath.

They interrogated the soul, 'Where are you coming from, human-killer, and where are you going, space-conqueror?'

The soul replied, saying, 'What binds me has been slain, and what surrounds me has been destroyed, and my desire has been brought to an end, and ignorance has died. In a world, I was set loose from a world and in a type from a type which is above and from the chain of forgetfulness which exists in time. From this hour on, for the time of the due season of the aeon, I will receive rest in silence.'

After Mary had said these things, she was silent, since it

was up to this point that the Savior had spoken to her.

Desire tries to keep the soul from ascending by saying it belongs to the world below and the powers that rule it. In the soul's attempt to escape, it is claiming that it does not belong to the material world. Since Desire did not see the soul come down from the heavens, it assumes it must be from the material world. The soul says that Desire did not recognize it because Desire thinks that the garment of flesh is the true spiritual self. Desire has unwittingly admitted that it never knew the soul's true self by saying it didn't see it descend. The response of the soul unmasks the blindness of Desire and the soul passes on.

When to himself his form appears unreal as do on waking all the forms he sees in dreams. When he has ceased to hear the many, he may discern the One--the inner sound which kills the outer.

And on page 15, it states:

If thy soul smiles while bathing in the Sunlight of thy Life; if thy soul sings within her chrysalis of flesh and matter; if thy soul struggles to break the silver thread that binds her to the Master: Know O Disciple, thy Soul is of the earth.

In the Gospel of Mary, the power of ignorance is judging. This gives us an insight into the nature of ignorance. It is judging others without knowing who or what they are. The soul has knowledge of that which ignorance knows nothing. It states that because everything in the lower world is to be dissolved, the powers of the transitory world have no real power over the eternal soul. It is because there is a body that there appears to be sin. Since flesh is impermanent, there is actually no sin, judgment, or condemnation. Again, the power itself gives a clue as to how to escape it by saying the soul is bound. The soul is innocent because it acts according to the nature of the spirit: it does not judge others or attempt to dominate anything or anyone.

The fourth power has seven forms – darkness, desire, ignorance, death, flesh, foolishness and wrath. Collectively, they are called "Wrath." Wrath says that the soul is a murderer because it has cast off the material body and a conqueror because it has traversed the spheres of the powers and overcome them. Again, the soul reinterprets the charges against it. The soul contrasts the subjection to material bonds — desire and ignorance — from which it has escaped, with the freedom of the timeless realm—silence and rest—to which it ascends. It conquers Wrath and moves on. At this point, Mary herself becomes silent and models the perfect rest of the soul that has been set free.

During Mary Magdalene's lifetime, views about the judgment of the dead were combined with the idea that angelic (or demonic) gatekeepers attempted to stop the souls and send them back into bodies. These notions were based on astrological beliefs that the planets were powers that governed the fate of all beings in the world. The soul's ascent was seen as an attempt to escape these arbitrary and unforgiving rules by successfully passing through each of the planetary spheres. Sinful souls were unable to escape and were returned to the flesh. Moral purity as well as preparation for the questions was necessary to reach the higher heavens.

The patriarchal model created by the Church defines women in terms of their sexual and relational roles to men: virgins, wives, mothers, widows, and prostitutes. The Church declared that Mary, Mother of Jesus symbolized the archetypal roles of "Virgin" and "Mother," and as Jesus, the Savior, could not possibly have a wife, the Church was unwilling to acknowledge Mary Magdalene as "Virgin" or "Mother." The role that was left was a prostitute, and it was assigned by Pope Gregory the Great.

In reality, the Gospel of Mary, other legends, and apocryphal works reveal Mary Magdalene as spiritual teacher, interlocutor, and close confidant of Jesus during his ministry on earth. The excerpt from her Gospel, explored earlier in this article, shows that her message is similar to that of Blavatsky and other great esoteric teachers. This view of Mary Magdalene places her in a new role or archetype—that of the "Teacher" or "Savior." Mary Magdalene was more than just a student or disciple of Christ, she embodied his teaching and had a powerful message of her own to share.

5

Hermit of the Caves

The Final Years

Mary Magdalene and the disciple Sidonius leave Lazarus in Massilia, where he becomes its first bishop, and travel northward, following the Huveaune river until they reach its source in the hills that would become known as La Sainte Baume. The immense natural cave they discover in the rocks, the size of a large house, becomes the new home of Mary Magdalene. Some miles down the valley was the village bearing the Roman name of Villalata that in centuries to come would be known as Saint-Maximin-La-Sainte-Baume.

The magnificent cave-grotto must have been even more

out of the way then it is to the pilgrim of today. It is here in this hermitage that Mary Magdalene spends the next 30 years of her life in solitude, in meditation and contemplation. But her solitude is only that of the world, for seven times a day angels came down to the cave and took her to the top of the hill where she is given the grace to hear the music and songs that are the sounds of heaven. From this height, the view stretches as far as the Mediterranean, and overlooks the surrounding forest, hills and valleys. On a clear day, one can visualize right across the sea, the coast of Africa; and further east, Palestine. It is presumed that she is here often drawn into ecstasy, although details of which are not in the written record.

The record does state however that she neither ate nor drank for the thirty years that she lived in the grotto. It is also presumed that during her 30 years as a hermitess in the cave of La-Sainte-Baume, she suffered and sacrificed in reparation not only for her own sins, but also as a soul victim for others, and that the early Church benefitted greatly from her sacrificial life of penances and mortifications, offered in union with her beloved Jesus, for the sake of His Church.

Following 30 years spent in prayer and longing to be reunited with Jesus, the day came when Jesus enlightened her that death was approaching, and He guided her down the hill toward the village of Villalata. On the way there (and a pillar still marks the place), she was met by Maximin who had been divinely inspired to go to meet her and lead her to his church. Once there, having received holy communion from his hand, she falls lifeless before the altar. The date was July 22, around the year 72 A.D.

Saint Maximin ordered her body to be interred with great dignity and pomp, and commanded that he himself be buried near her tomb after his death. And such was her beauty in the eyes of the Lord that during seven days the oratory was filled with the holy perfume of her sanctity.

One of the earliest documents on the life of Mary Magdalene after the death of Christ is a text in Latin, by an anonymous author. It dates back to the fifth or sixth century. In part, it reads as follows:

"After the glory of the Resurrection of Jesus Christ, the triumph of his Ascension, and the coming of the Holy Spirit, the word of God was spread far and wide, and the number of the faithful grew day by day. But the Priests of the Jews, the Pharisees and Scribes, kindled the fire of persecution, and chased most of Jesus' witnesses out of Judea. During the terrible persecutions, the disciples traveled to different places of the world to announce the Good News to the Gentiles.

One of the 70 disciples was Maximin, known for his perfection in moral integrity, illustrious through his doctrine, and honored for the gift he had been granted to perform miracles.

In the same manner as the Blessed Mother was placed in the care of John, so Mary Magdalene was placed in the care of Maximin, attentive to his religious guidance.

This is how, during the dispersion, Mary Magdalene left all her possessions and traveled to the sea, where in the company of Maximin, she boarded a vessel and safely arrived near the port of Marseille [France].

There, inspired by the Lord, they made their way to the town of Aix, and by their fasting, prayers, and through the spreading of the divine message, they attracted people to the cult of God, even though many were at first incredulous and not yet reborn through the waters of baptism.

Maximin governed the Church of Aix for numerous years, preaching the Word of God, chasing demons, anointing the dying, curing the blind and the crippled, and healing all manner of sickness.

When the time came for Mary Magdalene to be freed of her earthly body, she saw Christ who came to call her to the glory of the heavenly Kingdom. He came to give the substance of eternal life to the one who had so faithfully given of her substance when he walked the earth.

She died on the eleventh day before the Kalends of August, namely on July 22, amidst great rejoicing of the angels in heaven. Maximin embalmed her most holy body with many aromatic herbs, and placed it in an honorable tomb, over which he elevated a most beautiful church. There can be seen her white marble sarcophagus with sculptures that represent her story as to how she came to find the Lord at the house of Simon, and so obtained forgiveness of her sins, and the devout duties she carried out for the Savior's entombment."

Like many other ancient writings and works of art, this document has no signature. However, it indicates that the tradition of La-Sainte-Baume goes back to the earliest centuries of Christianity. Later in the 9th century, the martyrologist of King Alfred the Great of England, compiled all the known traditions and legends into a liturgical document. It contained some precisions on Mary Magdalene that confirmed the earlier Latin document, as seen by the following extracts:

"July 22 is the Feastday of Mary of Magdala, who had previously been a sinner plagued by seven demons. She came to see our Lord whilst he was at table in the house of a Jewish Pharisee, carrying a vase of precious perfumed ointment. And the Lord said to her: 'Your sins are forgiven, go in peace.'

Later she was chosen by Christ to witness his apparition at the Resurrection, the first of all mortals, and to announce his Resurrection to the Apostles.

After the Ascension, being torn with such terrible grief at his absence, she withdrew to a barren land where she remained for thirty years. Never in need of nourishment, God's angels came down seven times a day and transported her up to where she could hear the celestial music of heaven, and then carried her back to her grotto carved in the rock. It is for this reason that she was never hungry or thirsty.

And so it came to pass that after thirty years, a priest went to meet her in the desert and led her to his church. He gave her holy communion, whereafter she rendered her spirit to God, and the priest buried her. And many miracles took place at her tomb."

The two previous documents are historically important because of their description of the arrival of Mary Magdalene in ancient Gaul and the thirty years she spent in the cave grotto. The first was written before the Saracen invasion of France, and the second during the time the tomb and holy remains were concealed in the Church of Saint Maximin.

There were other documents relating to the life of Mary Magdalene in the Grotto of La-Sainte-Baume, but the most important ones that finally and definitely affirmed that the holy remains of Mary Magdalene were in Saint-Maximin, were the Bulls of Pope Boniface VIII, in 1295.

Miraculous Events

In the year 710, the Monks of the monastery of St Maximin were forced to flee their Monastery because of the invading Saracens (Moslem tribes from Arabia). They knew that they could not leave the holy remains of St Mary Magdalene for the invaders to destroy, so they devised a plan to move her remains into a more humble tomb next to the original as a disguise, and then bury the entire Chapel with earth and sand so that no part was visible.

Finally, the Arab occupation came to an end in the 10th century, but while the citizens remembered the events surrounding the burial of the Chapel and the tombs, the exact location was not known.

In 1279, Prince Charles II of Salerno, nephew of King Louis IX of France, resolved to find the tomb of Mary

Magdalene. Under the direction of a number of Church dignitaries and nobles, the search began in earnest, and workmen began the excavation work inside the church of Saint-Maximin and the land surrounding it.

The search continued for many days, and the prince himself joined in with the laborers removing mountains of earth. At last, they came upon a crypt that dated back to the 1st century.

The crypt was filled with earth and sand and they began removing this. On December 9, 1279, as Prince Charles was displacing the earth from the middle of the Crypt, the workmen digging on his right discovered a marble tomb buried deep in the sand. It was the sarcophagus-tomb of Sidonius, the one into which the holy remains of Mary Magdalene had been placed prior to the Monks fleeing in 710.

Before they were able to open it, a most marvelous fragrance rose up from the tomb that made all those present believe they had not found the treasure they were searching for.

On December 18, a number of Bishops, including the Archbishop of Arles and the Archbishop of Aix, came to Saint-Maximin, and in the name of the Church, officially witnessed the opening of the tomb.

The body was found to be complete except for a bone of the jaw that was missing. Among the dust particles at the bottom of the tomb, a small piece of cork was found. Inside it was a message written on parchment. It read:

"Year of the nativity of our Lord, 710, this sixth day of the month of December, under the reign of (not legible) and during the ravages of the Saracen nation, in fear of the Saracens, the body of the well-loved and venerable Mary Magdalene has been transferred, to be better concealed, from the alabaster tomb to the one in marble, out of which the body of Sidonius has been removed.'

The prince, overjoyed at having found the holy remains of Mary Magdalene, called together on May 5, 1280, in the town of Saint-Maximin, the prelates and a great number of religious of Provence and of France, together with the counts, barons, knights and persons of high rank in his kingdom and the nobles attached to his court, in order to proceed to the solemn elevation and translation of the relics.

The prelates having come to the tomb to remove the holy body, and while in the process of performing this venerable task, discovered a small ball of wax that contained a piece of bark. On it was a message more ancient than the parchment, and hardly legible. Written in Latin, it read:

"Hic requiescit corpus Mariae Magdalenae" (Here lies the body of Mary Magdalene)

The finding of this second testimonial caused great rejoicing among all those present and also the vast number of people outside who had come from many parts to assist at this solemn occasion.

There were several signs that were remarkable considering the body had been buried since the 1st century. It was found that the tongue still adhered to the mouth cavity, and from it had grown an aromatic plant. On seeing this marvel, the prince burst out into loud sobs. And overcome by deep emotion, he wept openly, bringing on the tears of many of those present.

The most remarkable sign of all was the small piece of skin that was found to be attached to the brow. It was smooth, clear, and lighter than the remainder of the body, and was the size of two fingertips. As it resembled live skin, it was subsequently named the "*Noli me tangere*" (Do not touch me)-the words spoken by Christ to Mary Magdalene at the Resurrection; it was believed to have been the touch of the risen Lord on the brow of Mary Magdalene.

This small particle of skin remained unchanged for another five hundred years, and no suitable explanation was ever found for the phenomenon. Five centuries after its discovery, it finally detached itself from the brow, and was placed in a separate reliquary.

Mary Magdalene is one of the first (if not *the* first) women mystics and hermits of the Church. Her cave-grotto with its remarkable view is now a large Chapel where Mass is celebrated each day. It houses an extraordinary reliquary containing part of her tibia bone and also the chapel boasts several beautiful statues and a beautiful altar. The Basilica of Saint Mary Magdalene in nearby Saint Maximin, Vézelay, France contains the tomb and the blessed remains of Saint Mary Magdalene. Since the 11th century the Basilica of St Mary Magdalene (known in French as Basilique Ste-Madeleine) in Vézelay has been one of the greatest European pilgrimage locations, especially during the middle ages. It is a large Basilica, only a few yards shorter that the great Notre-Dame Cathedral in Paris.

6

Mary Magdalene and the Egg

The Magdalene's travels eventually took Mary Magdalene to Rome, where because of her family's standing she was able to obtain an audience with the Roman Emperor, Tiberius Caesar. Her purpose was to protest to him that his governor in Judea, Pontius Pilate, and the two high priests, Annas and Caiaphas, had conspired and executed an innocent man, namely our Lord Jesus Christ.

She presented him with a red egg (representing the stone which had been rolled away), saying: "Christ is risen!" She told Caesar of Pilate's injustice toward Jesus. He responded by moving Pilate to Gaul, where he died under imperial displeasure after a prolonged illness. She then assisted St. John the Theologian in Ephesus. She preached boldly the gospel of the Risen Lord whom she loved.

According to the tradition, everyone visiting the Emperor was supposed to bring him a gift. Rich and influential people, of course, brought expensive gifts whereas the poor offered whatever they could afford. Mary Magdalene took an egg to the Emperor's palace and handed it to Tiberius Caesar with the greeting: "Christ is risen!"

Tiberius Caesar, naturally, could not believe what he heard and responded to her: "How could anyone ever rise from the dead? It is as impossible as that white egg to turn red." While Tiberius was speaking these words, the egg in the hand of Mary Magdalene began changing color until it finally became bright red.

Thus the Pascha greeting -- in universal Christendom, both East and West -- has ever since remained "Christ is risen!" and it became traditional for Christians throughout the world to color eggs in red.

Mary Magdalene then went on to explain to Tiberius Caesar that the now-red egg symbolized life rising from a sealed chamber, a symbol that would have been understandable to a pagan Roman.

Caesar heard the formal complaint presented by Mary Magdalene, and also had received reports of soldiers under Pilate molesting and killing civilians in Judea. For this Pilate was exiled to Vienne in Gaul where he died an unpleasant death. Interestingly, Pilate's wife Procula Claudia who had a dream about Jesus the night before He was brought before her husband for trial, had become a very pious and devout Christian, and died a saint of the Christian Church.

Eastern Christian legends blended folklore and Christian beliefs and firmly attached the egg to the Easter celebration. A Polish legend tells of when Mary Magdalene went to the sepulchre to anoint the body of Jesus. She had with her a basket of eggs to serve as a repast. When she arrived at the sepulchre and uncovered the eggs, lo, the pure white shells had miraculously taken on a rainbow of colors.

One legend concerns Mary, the Mother of Christ, known as the Theodokos among early Christians. It tells of the time the Blessed Virgin gave eggs to the soldiers at the cross. She entreated them to be less cruel and she wept. Her tears fell upon the eggs, spotting them with dots of brilliant color.

Decorating and coloring eggs for Easter was the custom in England during the Middle Ages. The household accounts of Edward I, for the year 1290, recorded an expenditure of eighteen pence for four hundred and fifty eggs to be gold-leafed and colored for Easter gifts.

7

The Gospel according to Mary Magdalene

Chapter 4

(Pages 1 to 6 of the manuscript, containing chapters 1 - 3, are lost. The extant text starts on page 7...)

. . . Will matter then be destroyed or not?

22) The Savior said, All nature, all formations, all creatures exist in and with one another, and they will be resolved again into their own roots.

23) For the nature of matter is resolved into the roots of its own nature alone.

24) He who has ears to hear, let him hear.

25) Peter said to him, Since you have explained everything to us, tell us this also: What is the sin of the world?

26) The Savior said: There is no sin, but it is you who make sin when you do the things that are like the nature of adultery, which is called sin.

27) That is why the Good came into your midst, to the essence of every nature in order to restore it to its root.

28) Then He continued and said, That is why you become sick and die, for you are deprived of the one who can heal you.

29) He who has a mind to understand, let him understand.

30) Matter gave birth to a passion that has no equal, which proceeded from something contrary to nature. Then there arises a disturbance in its whole body.

31) That is why I said to you, Be of good courage, and if you are discouraged be encouraged in the presence of the different forms of nature.

32) He who has ears to hear, let him hear.

33) When the Blessed One had said this, He greeted them all, saying, Peace be with you. Receive my peace unto yourselves.

34) Beware that no one lead you astray saying Lo here or lo there! For the Son of Man is within you.

35) Follow after Him!

36) Those who seek Him will find Him.

37) Go then and preach the gospel of the Kingdom.

38) Do not lay down any rules beyond what I appointed you, and do not give a law like the lawgiver lest you be constrained by it.

39) When He said this He departed.

Chapter 5

1) But they were grieved. They wept greatly, saying, How shall we go to the Gentiles and preach the gospel of the Kingdom of the Son of Man? If they did not spare Him, how will they spare us?

2) Then Mary stood up, greeted them all, and said to her brethren, Do not weep and do not grieve nor be irresolute, for His grace will be entirely with you and will protect you.

3) But rather, let us praise His greatness, for He has prepared us and made us into Men.

4) When Mary said this, she turned their hearts to the Good, and they began to discuss the words of the Savior.

5) Peter said to Mary, Sister we know that the Savior loved you more than the rest of woman.

6) Tell us the words of the Savior which you remember

which you know, but we do not, nor have we heard them.

7) Mary answered and said, What is hidden from you I will proclaim to you.

8) And she began to speak to them these words: I, she said, I saw the Lord in a vision and I said to Him, Lord I saw you today in a vision. He answered and said to me,

9) Blessed are you that you did not waver at the sight of Me. For where the mind is there is the treasure.

10) I said to Him, Lord, how does he who sees the vision see it, through the soul or through the spirit?

11) The Savior answered and said, He does not see through the soul nor through the spirit, but the mind that is between the two that is what sees the vision and it is [...]

(pages 11 - 14 are missing from the manuscript)

Chapter 8

. . . it.

10) And desire said, I did not see you descending, but now I see you ascending. Why do you lie since you belong to me?

11) The soul answered and said, I saw you. You did not see me nor recognize me. I served you as a garment and you did not know me.

12) When it said this, it (the soul) went away rejoicing greatly.

13) Again it came to the third power, which is called ignorance.

14) The power questioned the soul, saying, Where are you going? In wickedness are you bound. But you are bound; do not judge!

15) And the soul said, Why do you judge me, although I have not judged?

16) I was bound, though I have not bound.

17) I was not recognized. But I have recognized that the All is being dissolved, both the earthly things and the heavenly.

18) When the soul had overcome the third power, it went upwards and saw the fourth power, which took seven forms.

19) The first form is darkness, the second desire, the third ignorance, the fourth is the excitement of death, the fifth is the kingdom of the flesh, the sixth is the foolish wisdom of flesh, the seventh is the wrathful wisdom. These are the seven powers of wrath.

20) They asked the soul, Whence do you come slayer of men, or where are you going, conqueror of space?

21) The soul answered and said, What binds me has been slain, and what turns me about has been overcome,

22) and my desire has been ended, and ignorance has died.

23) In a aeon I was released from a world, and in a Type from a type, and from the fetter of oblivion which is transient.

24) From this time on will I attain to the rest of the time, of the season, of the aeon, in silence.

Chapter 9

1) When Mary had said this, she fell silent, since it was to this point that the Savior had spoken with her.

2) But Andrew answered and said to the brethren, Say what you wish to say about what she has said. I at least do not believe that the Savior said this. For certainly these teachings are strange ideas.

3) Peter answered and spoke concerning these same things.

4) He questioned them about the Savior: Did He really

speak privately with a woman and not openly to us? Are we to turn about and all listen to her? Did He prefer her to us?

5) Then Mary wept and said to Peter, My brother Peter, what do you think? Do you think that I have thought this up myself in my heart, or that I am lying about the Savior?

6) Levi answered and said to Peter, Peter you have always been hot tempered.

7) Now I see you contending against the woman like the adversaries.

8) But if the Savior made her worthy, who are you indeed to reject her? Surely the Savior knows her very well.

9) That is why He loved her more than us. Rather let us be ashamed and put on the perfect Man, and separate as He commanded us and preach the gospel, not laying down any other rule or other law beyond what the Savior said.

10) And when they heard this they began to go forth to proclaim and to preach.

Made in the USA
Las Vegas, NV
19 July 2023

74961469R00049